ABOUT ALL AFRICAN STATES AND PEOPLE

BABY PROFESSOR

EDUCATION KIDS

Learn about

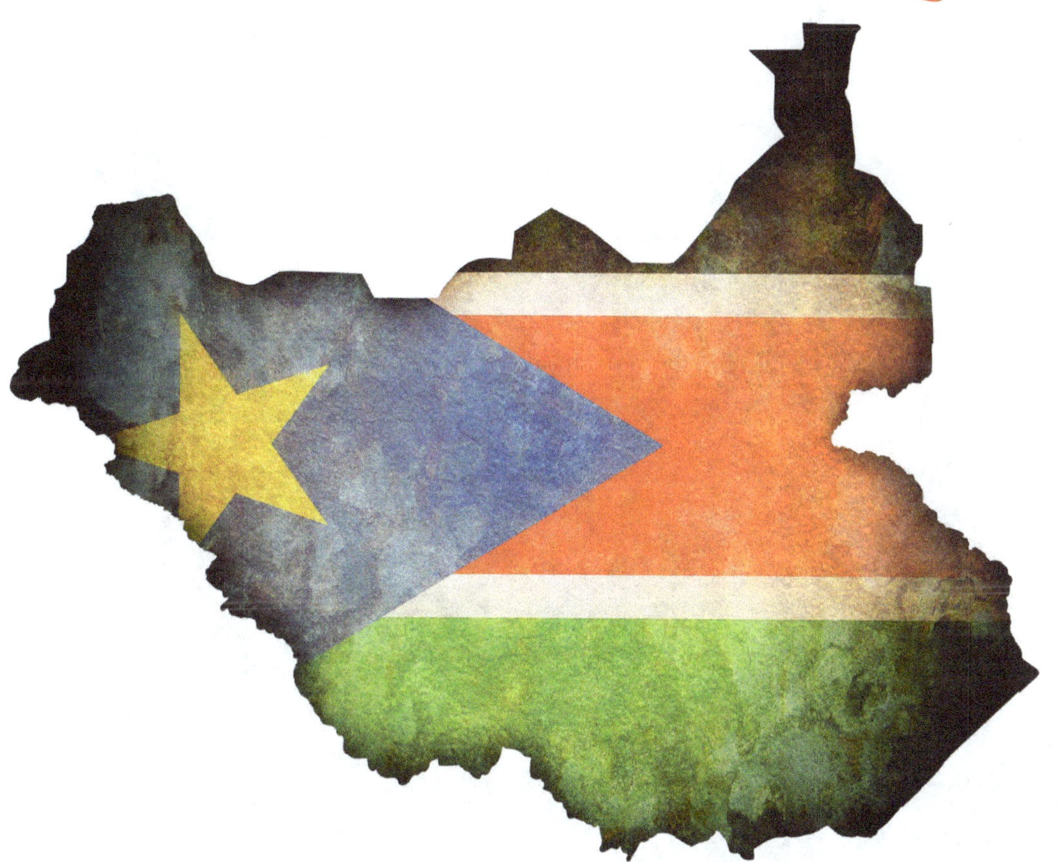

AFRICA

AFR

The first humans, and the first civilizations, began in Africa. The Pharaonic civilization of ancient Egypt is one of the world's oldest and longest-lasting civilizations. Cave paintings have been found in South Africa that are over 75,000 years old.

Long before humans emerged, Africa was attached to all the other continents to form one massive landmass called Pangea. Over millions of years Pangea slowly broke apart to form the world's continents as we know them today.

...TINENTAL DRIFT

AFTER

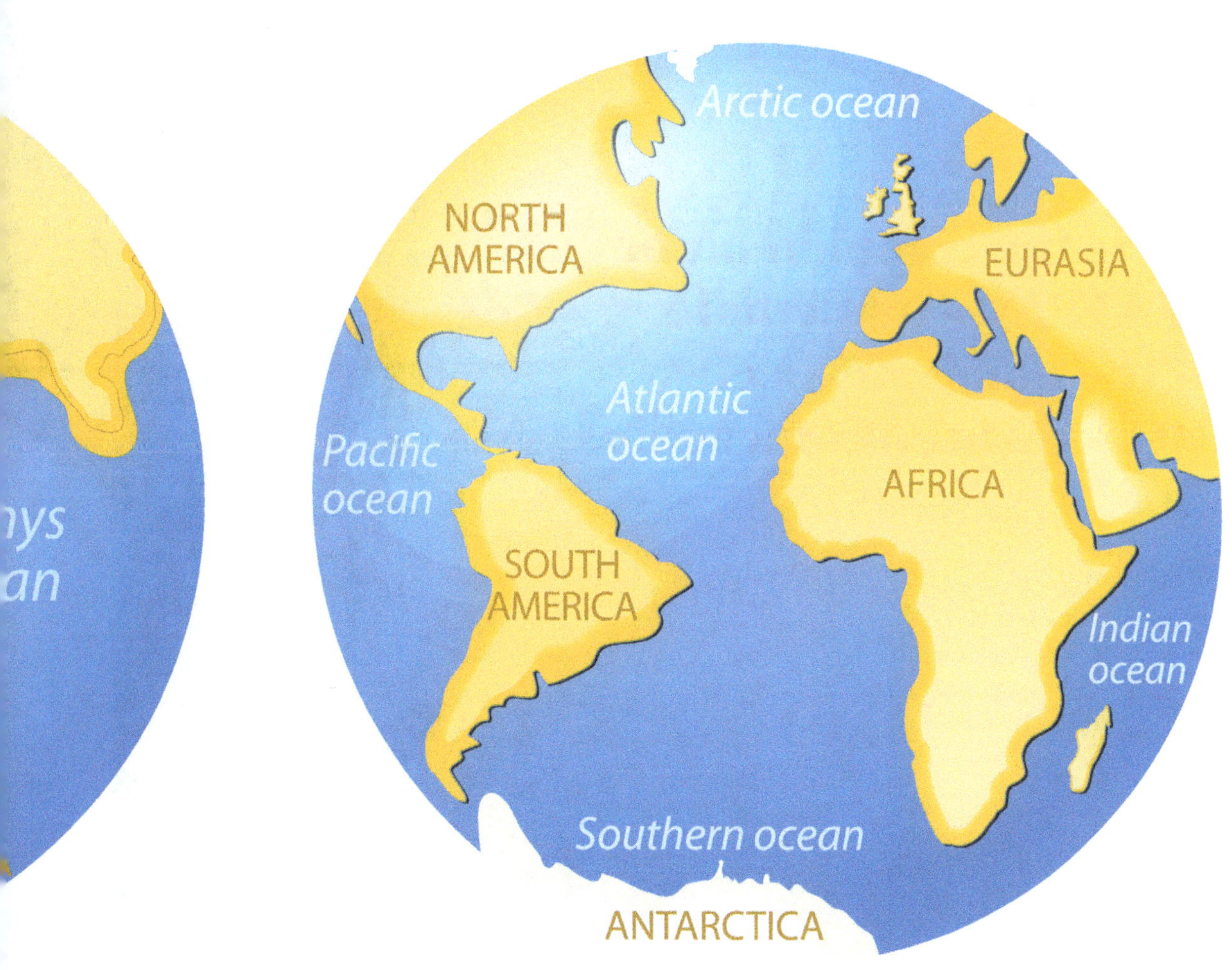

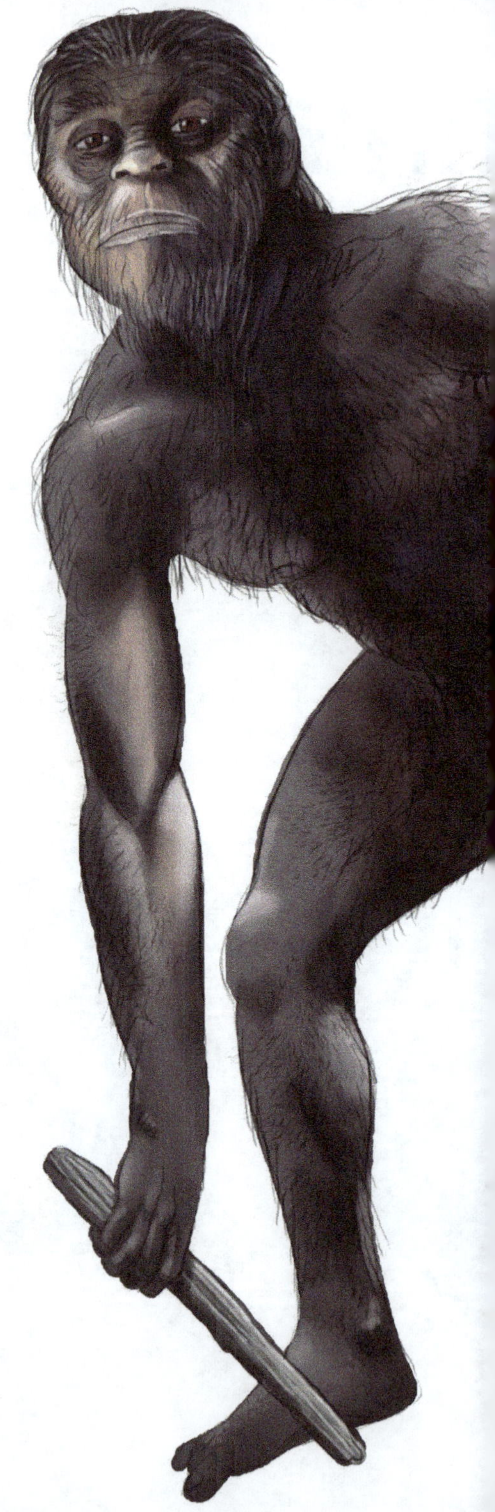

Lucy is the common name
of AL 288-1. A female
of the hominin species
Australopithecus afarensis.

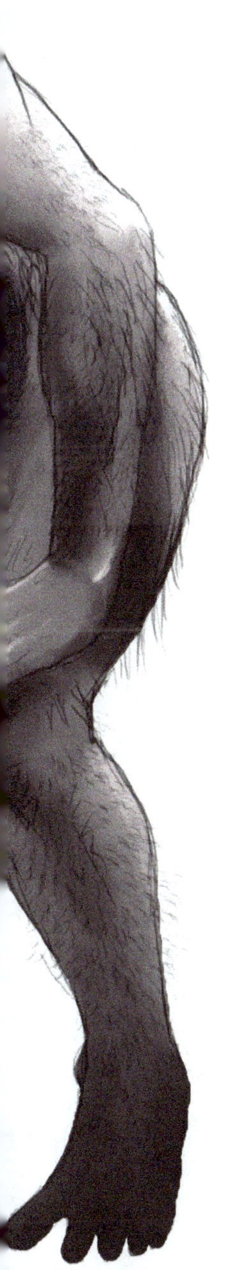

The oldest
human remains
discovered so
far were found
in Ethiopia.
The remains
are roughly
200,000 years
old. Africa is the
world's oldest
populated area.
Africa is where
human beings
first appeared on
earth.

Africa has the most countries of any continent. It has 54 countries and one non-self governing territory, the Western Sahara. It is the second largest and second most heavily populated continent.

Almost all of Africa was colonized by European powers during the 18th and 19th centuries, except Ethiopia and Liberia. Before colonial rule, Africa had up to 10,000 different states and autonomous groups with distinct languages and customs.

Today, Africa is united under a political organization known as the African Union (AU). The AU was established in 2001. Only Morocco is not a member of the AU.

One quarter of the world's languages are spoken only in Africa, with over 2,000 documented languages. South Africa is called the "Rainbow Nation" partly because it has 11 official languages spoken by people of many different races.

Islam is the dominant religion in Africa. Christianity is the second largest. Arabic is the most widely-spoken language. By 2050, about 38% of all the world's Christians will be living in Sub-Saharan Africa (SSA).

Half of all Africans are under the age of 25. Almost 40% of adults in Africa are illiterate and two-thirds of the population are women. The continent's population will double to 2.3 billion people by 2050.

Over 25 million people on Africa are HIV-positive and 17 million have died of AIDS. One in four adults in Swaziland is infected with HIV. Almost 90% of all cases of malaria worldwide occur in Africa.

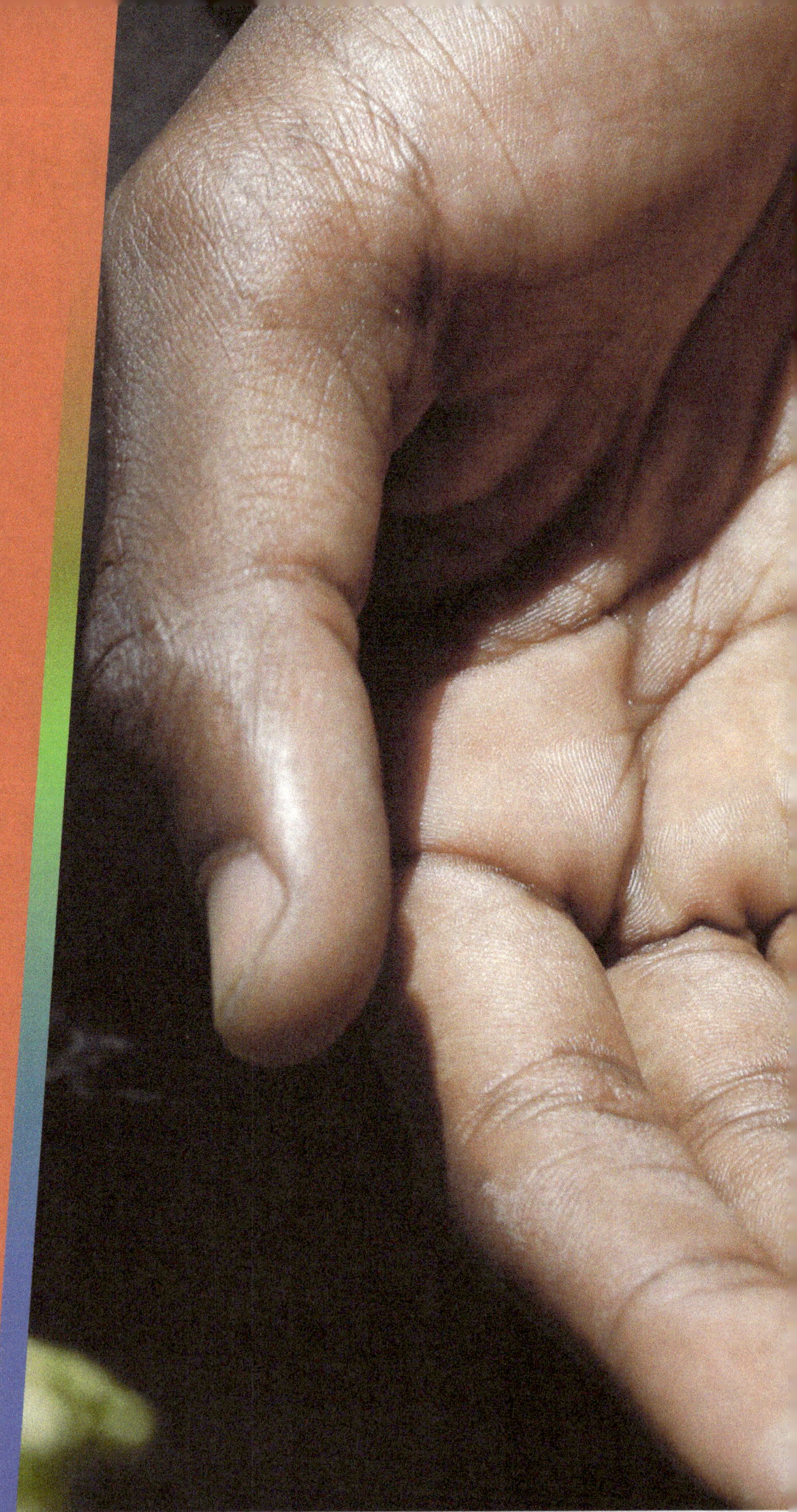

Here are some interesting facts in Africa. Tanzania has the world's highest Albinism. Women from Africa's Mursi tribe pierce their lips and wear plates as large as five inches across. A lone tribe in Kenya-called the "Kalenjin" has the fastest long-distance runners in the world.

More people speak French in Africa than there are people in France. The most popular sports in Africa are soccer and cricket. Both sports were introduced during the colonial era. Timbuktu, Mali is home of one of the oldest universities in the world, established in 982 CE.

In Africa, people have to walk an average of 3.7 miles daily to fetch water for various uses. About 41% of children in Africa aged between 5-10 years are actively involved in child labor. In Burundi, 39% of infants and toddler are underweight.

Africa is one of the most diverse places on the planet with a wide variety of terrain, wildlife, and climates. Its major natural areas are desert, savanna, and rain forest. Africa is full of natural beauty.

Africa is home to the world's largest living land animals, the African elephant and the giraffe. The hippopotamus is Africa's deadliest animal. Africa is rich with wildlife, including penguins, vultures, lions, cheetahs, seals, giraffes, gorillas, and crocodiles.

Giraffe by now are extinct in at least seven countries in Africa. There are no wild tigers in Africa, only in Asia. The hippopotamus kills more African people than do crocodiles and lions combined.

The fastest land animal in the world, the cheetah, lives in Africa. It is also a home to the world's largest reptile, the Nile crocodile. The world's largest primate, the gorilla, can also be found in the jungles of Africa.

Just as the people of Africa are diverse, so are the fish. Lake Malawi has more different fish species than any other freshwater system on earth. Africa's Lake Malawi has more than 500 varieties of fish.

Cairo is Africa's largest city. It is Egypt's capital and Egypt is Africa's most popular tourist destination. The country receives over 10 million visitors every year.

The Sahara is
the largest desert
in the world and
is bigger than
the continent of
North America.
Africa is the
world's second
driest continent
after Australia.
It is the hottest
continent on
earth too.

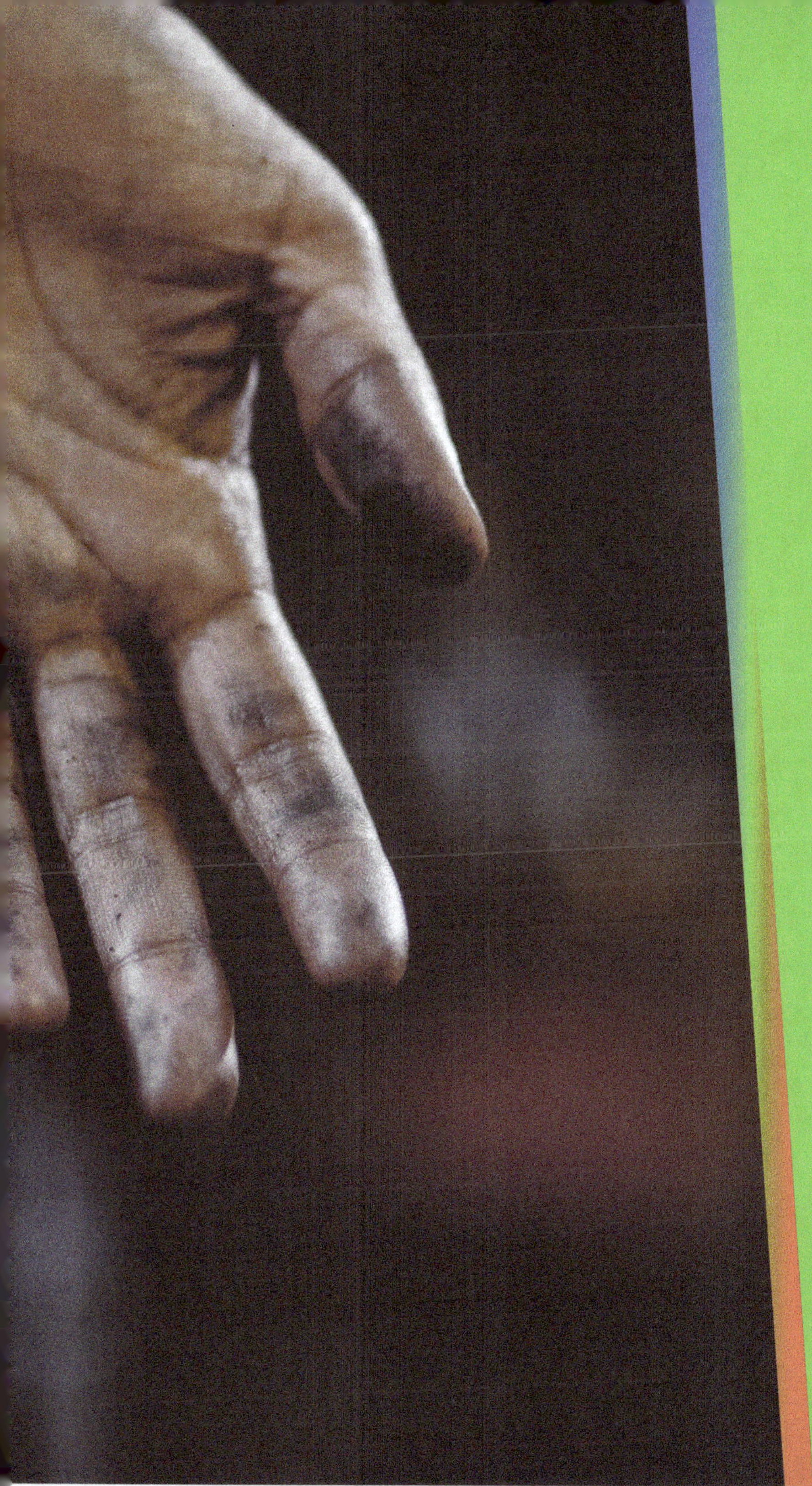

Africa has about
30% of the
earth's remaining
mineral
resources.
Nigeria is the
fourth largest
oil exporter
in the world.
Witwatersrand
in South Africa
produces almost
half of all the
gold mined in
Africa.

Lake Victoria is the largest lake in Africa and the second-largest freshwater lake in the world. The longest river in the world is the Nile River with a total length of 6,650 kilometers.

Madagascar is
the largest island
in Africa and the
fourth largest in
the world. It is in
the Indian Ocean
off the east coast
of Africa. The
lemur is only
found in the wild
in Madagascar.

Mount Kilimanjaro is the highest mountain in Africa. It is as high as 19,300 feet. It is so tall that glaciers can be found at its summit even though the mountain is near the equator. The Chagga people call Mt. Kilimanjaro home.

The Serengeti in Tanzania hosts the world's largest wildlife migration on Earth. There are over 750,000 zebra marching ahead of 1.2 million wildebeest as they cross this amazing landscape.

Africa has over 25% of the world's bird species. The word 'Africa' usually goes hand-in-hand with mental images of a vast savanna with animals of many different species living, eating, hunting, and resting.

Few people have internet connections in Africa. There are no more than 100 million Facebook users in all of Africa.

Africa is a home for 167 different species. We should protect their ecological niches to keep them from being endangered.